KEIRA KNIGHTLEY

KEIRA KNIGHTLEY

BIOGRAPHY

The Journey Of A Hollywood Icon
And Her Life Of Love And Talent

Collins Jefferson

KEIRA KNIGHTLEY

All rights reserved. No part of this publication may be reproduced, distributed, or transmitted in any form or by any means, including photocopying, recording, or other electronic or mechanical methods, without the prior written permission of the publisher, except in the case of brief quotations embodied in critical review and certain other noncommercial uses permitted by copyright law.

Copyright © Collins Jefferson 2024

KEIRA KNIGHTLEY

TABLE OF CONTENTS

INTRODUCTION

CHAPTER 1: WHO IS KEIRA KNIGHTLEY

1.1 Early Years

1.2 Family background

1.3 Discovering a love for acting

1.4 Childhood Influence

CHAPTER 2: BREAKING THROUGH WITH BEND IT LIKE BECKHAM

2.1 The Role That Changed Everything

2.2 Embracing Fame and Its Challenges

CHAPTER 3: SAILING THE HIGH SEAS: THE PIRATES OF THE CARIBBEAN ERA

3.1 Becoming Elizabeth Swann

3.2 Managing Stardom in a Blockbuster Franchise

CHAPTER 4: PERIOD DRAMA ROYALTY

4.1 Mastering Jane Austen: Pride and Prejudice

4.2 The Queen of Historical Fiction

CHAPTER 5: LOVE LIFE

5.1 Finding Romance in the Spotlight

5.2 Marriage and Motherhood

KEIRA KNIGHTLEY

CHAPTER 6: THE CRAFT OF ACTING
6.1 From Blockbusters to Indies
6.2 Transformative Roles
6.3 Challenging Projects

CHAPTER 7: PERSONAL GROWTH
7.1 Advocacy
7.2 Fighting for Women's Rights and Equality
7.3 Balancing Mental Health and Public Life

CHAPTER 8: LEGACY
8.1 A Lasting Impact on Cinema
8.2 Inspiring the Upcoming Generations

CONCLUSION

KEIRA KNIGHTLEY

INTRODUCTION

Hollywood is full of stars, but Keira Knightley stands out as one of the few who truly shines. Millions of people have been captivated by Keira's journey from a fiery young girl in Teddington, England, to a world-famous actress. She is a woman of immense talent, boundless grace, and quiet drive. Keira Knightley is more than just a famous actress. She is a writer, a trailblazer, and a woman who has been deeply passionate about her work and her life.

From her breakout role in Bend It Like Beckham, where she showed girl-next-door charm and unwavering determination, to her iconic role as Elizabeth Swann in the Pirates of the Caribbean movies, Keira's work has shown how versatile and tough she is. But her story doesn't end where the camera is. Aside from the costumes and plots, Keira's life has been filled with love—romantic, familial, and self-love—and a never-ending search for what makes her truly herself.

KEIRA KNIGHTLEY

This book goes behind the scenes of her meteoric rise and looks at the parts she played, the relationships she had, and the causes she cared about. It talks about her struggles with public attention, her victories over personal problems, and how she went from being a young, naive girl to a strong supporter of women's rights and mental health awareness.

We will reveal the many sides of a woman who has captivated people around the world—not just for her beauty, but also for her skill, honesty, and humanity—through vivid anecdotes, untold stories, and in-depth insights. Keira Knightley's life is more than a Hollywood fairytale; it's a plot of grit, grace, and an indomitable spirit.

Let's take a look into the life of Keira Knightley, who is an actress, a lawyer, a wife, a mother, and most of all, a star.

CHAPTER 1: WHO IS KEIRA KNIGHTLEY

Keira Knightley is a British actress celebrated for her skill, beauty, and versatility on screen. Born on March 26, 1985, in Teddington, England, she grew up in a creative home, with her father an actor and her mother a playwright. Knightley began acting at a young age, winning small parts in television and film before her breakout performance in the 2002 film Bend It Like Beckham.

Her portrayal of Elizabeth Swann in the Pirates of the Caribbean series catapulted her to international stardom, showing her ability to balance blockbuster appeal with nuanced performances. Known for her affinity for period dramas, Knightley has received critical acclaim for her roles in films such as Pride & Prejudice, Atonement, Anna Karenina, and The Imitation Game.

Beyond her acting work, Knightley is an outspoken advocate for gender equality, mental health awareness, and environmental sustainability. She has navigated the pressures of fame with grace, keeping a strong sense of individuality and purpose. As a wife, mother, and artist, Keira Knightley continues to inspire audiences around the world with her talent, resilience, and dedication to her craft.

1.1 Early Years

Keira Knightley was born in Teddington, a suburban town in southwest London. Raised in a family strongly rooted in the arts, her father, Will Knightley, was a stage and television actor, while her mother, Sharman Macdonald, was a playwright and former actress. Creativity and storytelling were central to her upbringing, and it was no surprise when Keira showed an interest in acting from a very young age.

Diagnosed with dyslexia at the age of six, Keira faced early difficulties with reading and academics. However, her determination to beat these obstacles became a defining trait. Her parents supported her goals, on the condition that she kept up with her schoolwork. By the age of three, she had already requested her t, showing her precocious drive to follow in her father's footsteps.

Her first acting opportunities came in television and commercials, where her natural talent and charm started to shine. Even as a child, she possessed a unique screen personality that set her apart. Keira's first notable film part came at the age of ten in Innocent Lies (1995), but her big break was still to come. These formative years were marked by persistence, family support, and a budding love for performing, all of which laid the foundation for her future success.

1.2 Family background

Keira Knightley comes from a family steeped in creativity and the performing arts, which profoundly influenced her job path. Her father, Will Knightley, is a respected British stage and screen actor with a

KEIRA KNIGHTLEY

long-standing career in theater. Her mother, Sharman Macdonald, is a playwright and former actor, best known for works such as When I Was a Girl, I Used to Scream and Shout. Together, her parents created an environment where artistic expression was encouraged and celebrated.

Keira has one older brother, Caleb, who has largely stayed out of the public eye, following his side acting Despite her family's involvement in the arts, they were cautious about exposing Keira to the pressures of the entertainment business. Her mother, in particular, played a pivotal role in shaping Keira's resilience and confidence, giving unwavering support as she navigated early challenges like dyslexia and the competitive world of acting.

The Knightley household was grounded in creativity but also humility, emphasizing the value of hard work and discipline. This balance helped Keira stay connected to her roots even as she achieved world stardom. Her family remains a cornerstone of her life, giving guidance and stability throughout her journey in the spotlight.

KEIRA KNIGHTLEY

1.3 Discovering a love for acting

Keira Knightley's love for acting emerged almost as early as she could talk. Growing up in a home immersed in the arts, her fascination with storytelling was inevitable. By the age of three, Keira had already voiced a desire for her own, inspired by watching her father perform on stage and hearing her mother's talks about plays and scripts. Acting, for Keira, was never a distant dream; it was a natural extension of her surroundings.

Her determination to pursue acting was obvious despite early challenges, including dyslexia, which made reading and learning lines difficult. However, her parents backed her ambition, fostering her love for performance while insisting she balance it with academics. Her first acting experiences came in school plays and small television roles, where she found not only a talent for acting but also a genuine love for the craft.

Keira's breakthrough moment in realizing her passion came during her part in the 1999 film Star Wars: Episode

I – The Phantom Menace, where she played Sabé, a decoy for Queen Amidala. Though a minor part, it offered her a glimpse into the possibilities of a film career. This exposure fueled her drive, and she began to see playing not just as a hobby but as her calling. From that point on, her focus sharpened, and her love for the art form became the cornerstone of her journey to stardom.

1.4 Childhood Influence

Keira Knightley's childhood was greatly influenced by her family's artistic background, which played a crucial role in shaping her future as an actress. Growing up in a home where creativity was the foundation of daily life, Keira was constantly surrounded by stories, performances, and conversations about theater and film. Her father, Will Knightley, a television and stage actor, and her mother, Sharman Macdonald, a playwright, were both important figures who introduced her to the world of performing arts from an early age.

KEIRA KNIGHTLEY

The artistic environment at home not only fostered Keira's love for acting but also helped her develop a deep knowledge of the craft. While her parents supported her passion, they remained cautious about the pressures of the entertainment business. They encouraged her to pursue her dreams, but only on the condition that she keep up with her schooling. This balance between artistic ambition and academic responsibility shaped Keira's strong work ethic and determination to achieve.

Keira's experiences with dyslexia had a significant effect on her childhood. She struggled with reading and writing, which made learning lines and schoolwork more difficult. However, rather than becoming discouraged, Keira used these hurdles to fuel her resilience. Her parents' support and her perseverance helped her navigate these difficulties, and her experiences with dyslexia only strengthened her desire to act, as it offered an outlet for her to express herself in ways that school often couldn't.

KEIRA KNIGHTLEY

In her early years, Keira was moved not only by her parents' work but also by the art of storytelling itself. The combination of her family's creative influence and her determination laid the foundation for a future that would eventually lead her to become one of the most respected actresses of her age.

CHAPTER 2: BREAKING THROUGH WITH BEND IT LIKE BECKHAM

Keira Knightley's breakthrough came in 2002 with the release of Bend It Like Beckham, a film that would not only introduce her to a global audience but also establish her as a rising star in Hollywood. The film, directed by Gurinder Chadha, tells the story of a young British-Indian girl, Jess Bhamra, played by Parminder Nagra, who dreams of becoming a professional soccer player despite her strict family's expectations. Keira played the part of Jules, Jess's best friend and soccer teammate, whose own ambitions and struggles with her mother's expectations mirrored Jess's journey.

At the time, Keira was only 17 years old, but her performance as the rebellious, confident Jules caught the attention of reviewers and audiences alike. Her natural charisma, athleticism, and ability to bring depth to her character made her stand out in a film filled with lively performances. For Keira, the part was a turning point—it allowed her to showcase her comedic timing, physicality, and emotional range, all while highlighting the challenges women face in usually male-dominated spaces like sports.

Although Bend It Like Beckham was a modest budget film, it became a surprise hit, grossing over $76 million internationally and gaining a cult following. The film's success not only propelled Keira into the spotlight but also won her critical acclaim. She was praised for her authenticity and likability, traits that would become key components of her on-screen persona in the years that followed.

For Keira, the experience of shooting Bend It Like Beckham was transformative. It marked the beginning of her transition from a young, unknown actress to a highly sought-after star. The film's success provided her with chances in bigger projects, and soon after, she would be cast in roles that would define her career, including Pirates of the Caribbean. Bend It Like Beckham proved to be more than just a breakout—it was the basis upon which Keira would build her Hollywood career, showcasing her ability to bring both charm and depth to diverse characters.

2.1 The Role That Changed Everything

The part that changed everything for Keira Knightley came in 2003 with Pirates of the Caribbean: The Curse of the Black Pearl. Cast as Elizabeth Swann, the spirited and resourceful daughter of the governor, Keira was thrust into a huge Hollywood blockbuster alongside Johnny Depp and Orlando Bloom. While the film was supposed to be a fun, adventurous ride, it quickly became much more—a global phenomenon, and with it, Keira's career skyrocketed.

Elizabeth Swann was a complex character—caught between her upper-class upbringing and her desire for adventure, courage, and freedom. Keira's portrayal of Elizabeth was both strong and vulnerable, showing her ability to balance wit and charm with a deep emotional

KEIRA KNIGHTLEY

range. Her performance resonated with audiences and critics alike, and her chemistry with Depp, who played the eccentric Captain Jack Sparrow, added layers of mystery and excitement to the story.

Before Pirates of the Caribbean, Keira had already established herself as a rising star, but it was this film that truly catapulted her into world recognition. The success of the movie, which grossed over $650 million internationally, turned Keira into a household name almost overnight. It wasn't just her physical presence or the iconic outfits she wore—it was her dynamic performance and the depth she brought to Elizabeth Swann that made her stand out in a sea of A-list actors.

The role marked a shift in Keira's career, as she moved from supporting parts in independent films and smaller productions to headlining big blockbusters. Her newfound fame also brought a level of scrutiny, with the media often focusing on her beauty and her supposed "girl-next-door" image. However, Keira maintained a sense of humility and groundedness, taking on new parts that continued to challenge her as an actress, even as she navigated the pressures of being one of Hollywood's hottest young stars.

Pirates of the Caribbean not only transformed Keira Knightley into an international sensation but also set the stage for a career defined by a variety of roles, critical praise, and a deep dedication to her craft. It was the part that truly changed everything—launching Keira into superstardom and establishing her as one of the most talented and versatile actresses of her generation.

2.2 Embracing Fame and Its Challenges

As Keira Knightley's fame skyrocketed following her success in Pirates of the Caribbean, she found herself thrust into the intense scrutiny that often follows global stardom. Though she had always dreamed of being an actor, the overwhelming attention that came with her newfound fame presented its own set of challenges. For Keira, navigating fame was never easy, as she quickly learned how invasive the public eye could be.

KEIRA KNIGHTLEY

The pressure to meet expectations, both professionally and personally, became increasingly obvious. Her every move, from the jobs she took on to her relationships, was dissected by the media. At the same time, she faced the constant comparison to other young actresses in Hollywood, often having to deal with headlines focused on her appearance and her supposed "girl-next-door" image. While the attention was flattering, Keira's desire for privacy and normalcy stayed steadfast.

To cope with the pressures of fame, Keira kept a sense of humility and distance from the industry's more superficial aspects. She became known for being down-to-earth, frequently emphasizing the importance of staying true to herself and her work. She was outspoken about the dangers of attention and the toll that it could take on one's mental health, especially for young women in Hollywood. Keira actively pushed back against the tabloid society, refusing to let the media define her on their terms.

KEIRA KNIGHTLEY

Keira also learned to embrace the positives that came with her fame—like the opportunities to work with world-renowned directors, the chance to play a diverse range of parts, and the platform it gave her to speak out on important issues. But she never let the glamour of Hollywood distract her from her ideals and the kind of actress—and person—she wanted to be. Fame, she learned, was fleeting, but her commitment to her craft and her integrity were what truly mattered.

Through this difficult journey, Keira grew into a more self-assured individual, balancing the demands of her work with a sense of personal responsibility. By embracing fame while maintaining her limits, Keira Knightley managed to thrive in an industry that often pressures its stars to conform, carving out a path that allowed her to stay true to her authentic self.

CHAPTER 3: SAILING THE HIGH SEAS: THE PIRATES OF THE CARIBBEAN ERA

The Pirates of the Caribbean era was a defining chapter in Keira Knightley's career, catapulting her into global stardom and cementing her position as a Hollywood icon. The series began with Pirates of the Caribbean: The Curse of the Black Pearl (2003), a swashbuckling adventure inspired by the Disney theme park ride. Keira was cast as Elizabeth Swann, a strong-willed, adventurous heroine who bucked the typical damsel-in-distress trope, holding her own among the likes of Johnny Depp's Captain Jack Sparrow and Orlando Bloom's Will Turner.

At just 17 years old, Keira was stepping into her first big Hollywood production. The part of Elizabeth Swann showed her versatility, blending vulnerability, intelligence, and determination. Whether commanding a pirate ship or navigating complex relationships, Keira brought depth and charm to a character that resonated with viewers worldwide. Her on-screen chemistry with Depp and Bloom added layers of tension and romance to the story, making her a standout in a star-studded group.

The success of the first film, which grossed over $650 million worldwide, led to the making of sequels Dead Man's Chest (2006) and At World's End (2007). In these films, Elizabeth evolved from a spirited noblewoman to a powerful leader, even assuming the part of Pirate King. This transformation allowed Keira to explore new facets of her character, from fierce action scenes to emotionally charged moments of love and loss.

However, the Pirates era was not without its difficulties. The massive scale of the productions and the relentless pace of shooting required both physical and emotional resilience. Keira often found herself making grueling stunts and working long hours on elaborate sets. Additionally, the skyrocketing fame that came with the franchise brought intense media scrutiny, something she managed with a mix of grace and drive.

The Pirates of the Caribbean films solidified Keira Knightley's place as a world superstar and introduced her to a new level of fame. Despite the commercial nature of the franchise, Keira's nuanced portrayal of Elizabeth Swann added depth to the films, showing that even in blockbuster roles, she could bring authenticity and complexity to her characters. The Pirates era remains a pivotal chapter in her career, one that showcased her skill, versatility, and ability to shine on the world stage.

3.1 Becoming Elizabeth Swann

Becoming Elizabeth Swann marked a transformative moment in Keira Knightley's career, as she stepped into one of her most iconic parts in Pirates of the Caribbean: The Curse of the Black Pearl (2003). At just 17 years old, Keira was cast as the spirited governor's daughter who defied societal norms, showing herself as a brave

KEIRA KNIGHTLEY

and capable force in a world dominated by pirates and adventure.

Elizabeth Swann was not your typical damsel in trouble. From the start, she stood out as a character of strength, intelligence, and determination. Her journey began as a curious young woman yearning for freedom from the constraints of her privileged life, but she quickly evolved into a formidable figure who could handle the high seas and hold her own in dangerous situations. For Keira, this role was a chance to showcase her ability to blend vulnerability with fierce independence. She brought Elizabeth to life with a perfect mix of elegance and grit, earning praise for her performance.

Preparing for the role required Keira to accept both the physical and emotional demands of the character. She trained in sword fighting, learned to perform stunts, and adapted to the grueling conditions of shooting on ships and remote locations. Despite her relative inexperience in big Hollywood productions, Keira's professionalism and dedication impressed her co-stars and the

KEIRA KNIGHTLEY

filmmakers. Her chemistry with Johnny Depp's eccentric Captain Jack Sparrow and Orlando Bloom's earnest Will Turner added layers of intrigue and romance to the story, making Elizabeth a key figure in the series.

Elizabeth's arc across the Pirates of the Caribbean trilogy allowed Keira to explore a range of feelings and experiences. From her initial part as a rebellious noblewoman to becoming the Pirate King in At World's End (2007), Elizabeth grew into a leader and warrior, embodying resilience and empowerment. Keira's portrayal resonated with audiences worldwide, solidifying Elizabeth Swann as one of the most memorable characters in modern film.

The part of Elizabeth Swann not only launched Keira into international stardom but also established her as a versatile actress capable of carrying both action-packed blockbusters and complex character-driven narratives. For Keira, becoming Elizabeth Swann was more than a career milestone—it was a defining moment that showed her ability to inspire and captivate on a global scale.

KEIRA KNIGHTLEY

3.2 Managing Stardom in a Blockbuster Franchise

Managing stardom in a blockbuster franchise like Pirates of the Caribbean was a life-changing experience for Keira Knightley, both professionally and emotionally. At just 17 years old when she was cast as Elizabeth Swann, Keira went from being a rising actor to an international sensation almost overnight. While the part gave her fame, fortune, and acclaim, it also introduced challenges that tested her resilience and determination.

The global success of Pirates of the Caribbean: The Curse of the Black Pearl in 2003, followed by its equally successful sequels, launched Keira into the spotlight. Suddenly, she was a household name, with her picture plastered on posters, magazine covers, and fan merchandise. For an actress so young, managing the intense attention was overwhelming. The media's fixation on her looks and private life often overshadowed her work, making her a target for tabloid scrutiny. Keira later spoke candidly about how the pressures of fame, especially the relentless criticism of her appearance, took a toll on her mental health.

Working on a blockbuster series also came with a grueling schedule and demanding conditions. Filming the Pirates movies meant long hours on elaborate sets, often under trying weather conditions. Keira performed many of her stunts, from sword fighting to navigating ship riggings, which took extensive physical preparation. Despite these demands, she stayed professional and committed to delivering her best performance in every scene.

To handle the pressures of stardom, Keira leaned on her family and a close-knit circle of friends for support. She also made a conscious effort to maintain a feeling of normalcy in her life, keeping her world separate from her public persona. Keira used her downtime between films to work on smaller, more personal projects, ensuring that her career wasn't defined solely by her involvement in the franchise.

KEIRA KNIGHTLEY

Over time, Keira found ways to balance the opportunities and challenges that came with being part of a big Hollywood series. She embraced the lessons the franchise taught her about acting, teamwork, and resilience, while also learning to set limits to protect her mental and emotional well-being. Managing stardom in the Pirates of the Caribbean series was a defining chapter in Keira Knightley's life, shaping her into an actress who could easily navigate both the highs and lows of fame.

KEIRA KNIGHTLEY

CHAPTER 4: PERIOD DRAMA ROYALTY

Keira Knightley has become synonymous with period plays, earning her the unofficial title of "period drama royalty." With her striking features, refined elegance, and remarkable ability to inhabit characters from bygone times, Keira has become a master of bringing historical figures and fictional heroines to life. Her work in this genre is marked by highly acclaimed performances in films that combine lush settings, intricate costumes, and compelling narratives.

Keira's ascent in the world of period plays began with her Oscar-nominated portrayal of Elizabeth Bennet in Joe Wright's adaptation of Pride & Prejudice (2005). Taking on one of literature's most beloved heroines, Keira gave a spirited performance that captured Elizabeth's wit, intelligence, and fierce independence. Her work in this film showed her ability to blend modern sensibilities with the nuanced emotional depth needed for historical characters.

Following this, Keira continued to shine in period films, each adding to her reputation in the genre. In Atonement (2007), also directed by Joe Wright, she played Cecilia Tallis, a woman stuck in a tragic love story during the 1930s. Her performance, paired with the film's sweeping visuals, became one of her most memorable parts. Keira also starred in The Duchess (2008), portraying Georgiana Cavendish, a complex and charismatic figure in 18th-century England, further solidifying her image as a leading lady in historical dramas.

Keira's affinity for period films isn't limited to romantic dramas; she's also explored historical figures in more intense settings. In Anna Karenina (2012), she took on the titular part in Tolstoy's classic tale of love and tragedy, giving a mesmerizing performance that balanced passion and vulnerability. In The Imitation Game (2014), Keira played Joan Clarke, a brilliant mathematician working alongside Alan Turing during World War II. Her

KEIRA KNIGHTLEY

performance earned her another Academy Award nomination and showed her range within the genre.

What sets Keira apart in the world of period dramas is her ability to bring authenticity and relatability to her characters, no matter the historical setting. Her expressive performances make audiences feel the timeless feelings of love, ambition, heartbreak, and resilience. Combined with her keen eye for projects with strong storytelling and her collaboration with visionary directors, Keira has won her place as a luminary in period films.

For fans of historical films, Keira Knightley's name has become synonymous with the beauty, complexity, and emotional depth that define the very best of the genre. Her ongoing contributions to period dramas continue to solidify her standing as royalty in this unique and challenging cinematic space.

KEIRA KNIGHTLEY

4.1 Mastering Jane Austen: Pride and Prejudice

Keira Knightley's portrayal of Elizabeth Bennet in Joe Wright's Pride & Prejudice (2005) remains one of the most celebrated adaptations of Jane Austen's classic book. Taking on the part of one of literature's most beloved and fiercely independent heroines was no small task, especially considering the long shadow cast by previous portrayals. However, Keira's interpretation breathed new life into Elizabeth, giving a modern yet authentic perspective that resonated with audiences and critics alike.

From the moment she appears on screen, Keira catches Elizabeth's sharp wit, fiery intelligence, and unyielding spirit. Her performance is nuanced, balancing Elizabeth's playful humor with times of deep vulnerability. Keira's Elizabeth is not simply a product of her time but a relatable, timeless character whose battles with class, love, and personal growth feel as relevant today as they did in Austen's era. Her chemistry with Matthew

KEIRA KNIGHTLEY

Macfadyen, who played the brooding Mr. Darcy, brought a fresh intensity to one of literature's most famous romance dynamics, making their love story both electric and tender.

Joe Wright's idea for the film was rooted in emotional authenticity and a raw, natural aesthetic. Keira embraced this direction, giving a performance that felt grounded yet brimming with energy. She made Elizabeth's defiance of social norms and her refusal to compromise her values feel real and modern without losing the historical essence of the character. Her sharp, expressive delivery of Austen's dialogue added a vibrant edge to the film, endearing her to fans of the book and newcomers alike.

The part won Keira her first Academy Award nomination for Best Actress, solidifying her as one of Hollywood's most talented and versatile performers. Critics praised her ability to balance Elizabeth's strength with her softer, more romantic side, creating a fully realized character that stood out even in the setting of an ensemble cast.

KEIRA KNIGHTLEY

Keira's success in Pride & Prejudice marked a turning point in her career, establishing her as a master of period plays and a capable leading lady. The film's acclaim and enduring popularity introduced Jane Austen's world to a new generation and reinforced Keira's standing as a force to be reckoned with in historical cinema.

Through Pride & Prejudice, Keira Knightley didn't just master Jane Austen—she redefined what it means to bring one of her most iconic characters to life, leaving an indelible mark on both her career and the memory of Elizabeth Bennet.

4.2 The Queen of Historical Fiction

Keira Knightley has won her reputation as the "Queen of Historical Fiction," a title that shows her extraordinary ability to bring history's most complex characters and eras to life on screen. With a mix of timeless elegance, emotional depth, and an innate understanding of the human stories behind the historical settings, Keira has

KEIRA KNIGHTLEY

become one of the most recognized faces in period dramas and historical films.

Her journey in historical fiction began with her breakthrough performance in Pride & Prejudice (2005), where she expertly embodied Jane Austen's Elizabeth Bennet. Keira's portrayal captured the intelligence, wit, and defiance of a woman challenging societal norms, earning her an Academy Award nomination and setting the stage for a career defined by compelling roles in historical film. This part established Keira as a natural fit for stories set in the past, where her ability to balance strength and vulnerability shines.

Over the years, Keira has delivered memorable performances across a range of historical periods. In Atonement (2007), she played Cecilia Tallis, a woman caught in a tragic love story during World War II, bringing emotional intensity to a tale of loss and redemption. In The Duchess (2008), Keira captured the complex life of Georgiana Cavendish, the Duchess of Devonshire, a figure of both public adoration and private pain in 18th-century England. These parts showed her versatility in depicting characters navigating the challenges of their time, from societal pressures to personal heartbreak.

Keira's ability to bring gravitas and authenticity to historical fiction goes beyond romance and drama. In The Imitation Game (2014), she played Joan Clarke, a pioneering mathematician and cryptanalyst during World War II. This part not only showed her range but also highlighted her commitment to telling stories of strong, trailblazing women who shaped history. Similarly, her portrayal of Anna Karenina (2012) in the lavish adaptation of Tolstoy's book showed her talent for capturing the passion and tragedy of a character caught in the tumult of her desires.

Keira's success in historical fiction is not merely about her ability to wear corsets and manage opulent sets. It's her understanding of the emotional core of these stories—the love, ambition, resilience, and pain that transcend time—that makes her performances resonate

KEIRA KNIGHTLEY

with current audiences. She brings a contemporary sensibility to historical figures, making them feel relevant and alive while respecting the authenticity of their eras.

As the queen of historical fiction, Keira Knightley continues to redefine what it means to tell stories of the past, ensuring that these tales remain as vibrant and captivating as the eras in which they are set.

CHAPTER 5: LOVE LIFE

Keira Knightley's love life has been characterized by her choice for privacy, grace, and a down-to-earth approach despite her immense fame. In a world where the personal lives of celebrities are often thrust into the spotlight, Keira has successfully managed to keep much of her romantic journey out of the tabloids, allowing her relationships to grow away from public scrutiny.

In the early 2000s, Keira's rising stardom saw her romantically linked with a few famous names. She had a high-profile relationship with actor Jamie Dornan, known today for his parts in Fifty Shades of Grey and The Fall. Their romance, which lasted for about two years, was often scrutinized by the media, giving Keira an early taste of how difficult it could be to maintain a private life under the spotlight. The pair parted ways amicably, with both going on to focus on their respective jobs.

KEIRA KNIGHTLEY

Keira later dated actor Rupert Friend, whom she met on the set of Pride & Prejudice. Their relationship lasted five years and was defined by its low profile, with the couple rarely making public appearances together. Despite their breakup in 2011, Keira and Rupert parted on good terms, showing her maturity and respect for her partners even as the relationship ended.

The most important chapter of Keira's love life began in 2011 when she started dating musician James Righton, a member of the indie band Klaxons. Unlike the glitzy romances often associated with Hollywood stars, Keira and James's relationship was based on mutual respect, humor, and a shared desire for a private life. The couple married in a low-key ceremony in Mazan, France, in 2013, choosing simplicity and closeness over extravagance.

Together, Keira and James have built a strong, supportive relationship. They have two daughters, born in 2015 and 2019, and Keira often talks about the joys and challenges of balancing motherhood with her work.

While she remains highly protective of her family's privacy, she has occasionally shared insights into her life as a parent, highlighting her commitment to providing a nurturing and grounded upbringing for her children.

Keira's love life represents her values: authenticity, privacy, and a focus on meaningful connections. Her enduring relationship with James Righton and their family life away from the spotlight shows that even in the whirlwind of Hollywood, it's possible to cultivate a life rooted in love, respect, and balance.

5.1 Finding Romance in the Spotlight

Finding romance in the spotlight has always been a delicate balance for Keira Knightley, a global star who values privacy in an industry that lives on exposure. Despite her celebrity status, Keira has managed to cultivate important relationships, often keeping them shielded from the public eye to preserve their authenticity.

KEIRA KNIGHTLEY

During her early years in the industry, Keira faced the challenges of dating in the limelight. Her relationship with actor Jamie Dornan in the mid-2000s was one of her first high-profile loves. Though the two were a glamorous pair, the constant media attention added strain to their relationship. Keira later reflected on the pressures of fame during that time, admitting how the spotlight can complicate even the most genuine relationships.

After her split with Dornan, Keira found love with Rupert Friend, her co-star from Pride & Prejudice. Their five-year relationship, while more private, still attracted public attention due to their shared star power. The couple's decision to keep a low profile helped Keira navigate the challenges of having a romantic relationship while being a prominent public figure.

Keira's most important romantic chapter began in 2011 when she met James Righton, a musician from the indie rock band Klaxons. Their friendship was refreshingly different from the Hollywood norm, characterized by its simplicity and mutual respect. The pair's bond quickly deepened, leading to their marriage in 2013. Their wedding in the south of France was a far cry from the lavish ceremonies typical of celebrity unions—an intimate and understated affair that mirrored their shared desire for a private life.

Being in the spotlight hasn't stopped Keira from building a strong and lasting bond with James. Together, they have navigated the ups and downs of fame while raising two girls. Keira has often spoken about the importance of her family, emphasizing that her home life offers a grounding force amid the chaos of her career.

Despite her celebrity, Keira has shown that it's possible to find true love in the spotlight by prioritizing trust, privacy, and shared values. Her journey shows that while fame can complicate relationships, it can also coexist with meaningful, enduring romance when approached with intention and care.

KEIRA KNIGHTLEY

5.2 Marriage and Motherhood

Keira Knightley's journey into marriage and motherhood reflects a life defined by love, balance, and her steadfast desire for privacy amidst the demands of global fame. Her relationship with musician James Righton, her husband since 2013, and her role as a devoted mother to their two daughters exemplify how she has gracefully navigated these highly personal milestones while keeping a flourishing career.

Keira met James Righton, a member of the indie band Klaxons, in 2011, introduced by common friends. Their relationship quickly bloomed, marked by a shared sense of humor, mutual respect, and a desire to keep their love life out of the public eye. In May 2013, the couple exchanged vows in a charming, low-key ceremony in Mazan, a picturesque town in the south of France. Keira's bridal look—a simple, elegant dress paired with a cropped Chanel jacket—perfectly encapsulated her understated approach to the event. The wedding,

KEIRA KNIGHTLEY

attended by close friends and family, showed their shared values of intimacy and authenticity.

Motherhood added another deep layer to Keira's life. The couple received their first daughter, Edie, in 2015, and their second child, Delilah, in 2019. Keira has been open about the joys and challenges of raising children while maintaining her job. She has candidly discussed the realities of motherhood, from sleepless nights to the emotional weight of balancing family life with work responsibilities. Her honesty about these experiences has resonated with many, highlighting the universal challenges and triumphs of parenthood.

As a mother, Keira is truly committed to providing her children with a grounded upbringing, away from the glare of Hollywood's spotlight. She and James have worked to maintain a stable, private family life in London, focusing on creating a nurturing environment for their girls. Keira has also used her platform to fight for issues affecting women and mothers, from the

KEIRA KNIGHTLEY

importance of paid parental leave to the societal pressures put on new mothers.

Through her marriage to James Righton and her role as a mother, Keira Knightley has proven that it's possible to achieve a fulfilling personal life alongside a demanding career. Her ability to value love, family, and self-expression while navigating the challenges of fame underscores her strength, grace, and unwavering sense of identity. Marriage and motherhood have not only enriched her personal life but have also deepened her knowledge of the parts she chooses to portray, adding layers of authenticity to her work as an actress and a storyteller.

CHAPTER 6: THE CRAFT OF ACTING

For Keira Knightley, the craft of acting is both an art and a deeply personal exploration of human feeling. From her earliest roles to her most famous performances, Keira has demonstrated an exceptional ability to immerse herself in her characters, blending technical precision with raw vulnerability. Her approach to acting shows a deep respect for storytelling and a relentless commitment to authenticity.

Keira's journey as an actress began at a young age, but it was her discipline and drive that set her apart. She handles every part with meticulous preparation, delving into the historical, social, and emotional contexts of her characters. Whether learning to sword fight for Pirates of the Caribbean, mastering the nuances of 18th-century royalty in The Duchess, or capturing the restrained intensity of Joan Clarke in The Imitation Game, Keira dedicates herself fully to understanding the world her characters inhabit.

KEIRA KNIGHTLEY

Her love for complex, layered characters is obvious in the roles she chooses. Keira often gravitates toward strong, independent women navigating adversity—characters who question social norms, fight for their desires or wrestle with moral dilemmas. From Elizabeth Bennet's defiance of convention in Pride & Prejudice to Anna Karenina's tragic pursuit of love, Keira brings depth and nuance to these portrayals, making them resonate with modern viewers.

Keira's acting style is marked by her ability to express a wide range of emotions with subtlety and intensity. She excels in times of quiet introspection, using her expressive eyes and body language to communicate her characters' inner turmoil. At the same time, she can give fiery, impassioned performances that command attention. This duality helps her to excel in both intimate character studies and grand historical epics.

Collaboration is a key part of Keira's craft. She has worked repeatedly with directors like Joe Wright, who

KEIRA KNIGHTLEY

share her commitment to rich, emotionally driven stories. Her willingness to trust her directors and co-stars, combined with her openness to creative risks, has led to some of her most acclaimed performances.

Keira also sees acting as a way of connecting with audiences on a universal level. She believes in the power of storytelling to promote empathy and understanding, and her work reflects this philosophy. By choosing parts that challenge her and resonate strongly with viewers, Keira has established herself as an actress who brings authenticity and humanity to every project.

For Keira Knightley, acting is not just about performance—it's about truth. Her dedication to the craft has not only defined her career but also inspired audiences and fellow actors alike, cementing her place as one of the most respected talents of her age.

KEIRA KNIGHTLEY

6.1 From Blockbusters to Indies

Keira Knightley's career trajectory has been marked by her ability to smoothly transition between major Hollywood blockbusters and smaller, more intimate independent films, proving her versatility and commitment to both commercial and artistic storytelling. While she is perhaps best known for her part as Elizabeth Swann in the Pirates of the Caribbean series, her body of work covers a broad range of genres, from epic period dramas to thought-provoking indie films.

Her breakthrough came with blockbuster parts that showcased her charm, ability, and captivating presence. The Pirates of the Caribbean series (2003–2017) solidified Keira as a global star, allowing her to showcase her ability in large-scale action films. As Elizabeth Swann, she held her own against the towering figures of Johnny Depp and Orlando Bloom, turning a supporting part into one of the franchise's most beloved characters. The success of Pirates of the Caribbean opened doors for Keira in Hollywood's biggest projects, including King Arthur (2004) and The Duchess (2008), where her elegance and emotional depth allowed her to shine in both historical epics and high-budget dramas.

Keira's desire to push herself artistically and avoid being pigeonholed as just a Hollywood star led her to explore the world of independent film. She transitioned to indie movies that were more intimate and character-driven, where her performances could be more subtle and nuanced. One such project was The Edge of Love (2008), a drama about the life of author Dylan Thomas, where Keira played his lover, Vera Phillips. While the film wasn't a major financial success, Keira's performance was widely praised for its vulnerability and complexity, marking a change from her blockbuster image to a more introspective and daring approach to acting.

In 2012, Keira starred in Anna Karenina, directed by Joe Wright, another big-budget historical drama, but the project's unique, experimental style—combining traditional cinematic methods with theatrical

KEIRA KNIGHTLEY

elements—felt like a departure from mainstream Hollywood. It was her part in smaller films like Begin Again (2013), where she portrayed a struggling singer-songwriter in New York, and Colette (2018), as the famous French author, that further cemented her place in the indie film scene. In both, Keira showed a natural ease with emotionally raw and complex parts, proving her range as an actress and her willingness to take risks.

Keira's ability to switch between the worlds of blockbusters and indies speaks to her broad playing range and her deep commitment to storytelling. While the glitz of Hollywood blockbusters gave her fame and financial stability, the indie films allowed her to experiment with more diverse and challenging characters, often in stories that push artistic limits. This balance between commercial success and artistic integrity has kept Keira's career dynamic and her performances fresh, allowing her to build a lasting legacy that resonates with viewers across genres.

By refusing to be typecast and embracing roles that span both mainstream and independent cinema, Keira Knightley has proven that an actress can thrive in both worlds, bringing depth and authenticity to every project, no matter its scale or budget.

6.2 Transformative Roles

Keira Knightley's career is defined by her transformative roles—performances that go beyond surface-level beauty to show the emotional complexity and depth of the characters she portrays. Whether she's navigating historical periods or exploring raw emotional landscapes, Keira has proven time and again that she has the range to fully inhabit diverse parts, delivering performances that resonate with audiences long after the credits roll.

One of the most important transformative moments in Keira's career came with her portrayal of Elizabeth Bennet in Pride & Prejudice (2005). While the character of Elizabeth was already beloved by readers of Jane Austen's book, Keira brought a fresh, modern sensibility to the role, infusing Elizabeth with a sharp wit, fierce independence, and a quiet emotional depth. Keira's Elizabeth was both mentally empowered and vulnerable, capturing the complexities of a woman who defies social expectations. This part marked a turning point in Keira's career, earning her an Academy Award nomination and establishing her as one of the most respected actresses of her age.

Keira's performance in Atonement (2007) further showed her ability to transform into characters that were far from the confident heroines she often portrayed. In this adaptation of Ian McEwan's book, Keira played Cecilia Tallis, a young woman whose life is irrevocably changed by a misunderstanding that leads to a tragic miscarriage of justice. Her portrayal was haunting, capturing both Cecilia's emotional restraint and the heartbreak of her love being torn apart. Keira's ability to convey the inner turmoil of her character through subtle expressions and small gestures earned her critical acclaim and solidified her standing as a dramatic powerhouse.

KEIRA KNIGHTLEY

In The Duchess (2008), Keira transformed once again, this time into the complicated, tragic figure of Georgiana Cavendish, the Duchess of Devonshire. Set in 18th-century England, the film covers Georgiana's tumultuous marriage to the Duke, as well as her relationships with her lover and her political activism. Keira's performance as the beautiful yet emotionally conflicted duchess displayed her ability to portray a woman caught between duty, love, and personal sacrifice. The part required her to display both regal elegance and raw vulnerability, making it one of her most layered performances.

In Colette (2018), Keira once again reinvented herself, portraying the French author Sidonie-Gabrielle Colette. Known for her groundbreaking works in the early 20th century, Colette was a woman ahead of her time, navigating a complex relationship with her controlling husband and fighting for respect in a male-dominated literary world. Keira fully accepted the part, shedding her usual refined demeanor for a more rebellious, defiant

KEIRA KNIGHTLEY

character who challenges societal norms. Her transformation into Colette was both physical and emotional, requiring her to accept the character's boldness and sexual liberation, and it won her widespread praise for her fearless portrayal of such a multifaceted figure.

Keira's work in The Imitation Game (2014) further showed her transformative abilities. As Joan Clarke, a brilliant cryptanalyst during World War II, Keira portrayed a woman whose intellect and accomplishments were overshadowed by her gender in a male-dominated field. Keira's portrayal of Joan was understated yet powerful, showing a woman of quiet strength who made difficult sacrifices in both her professional and personal life. Her performance in this supporting part was important in conveying the emotional complexity of a woman whose talents were often overlooked, and it earned her a second Academy Award nomination.

From period dramas to biographical roles, Keira Knightley's career has been defined by her ability to inhabit transformative roles that question the expectations of both her characters and her audience. She consistently takes on parts that demand both emotional vulnerability and intellectual depth, showcasing a versatility that has solidified her as one of the finest actresses of her age. Through each transformative performance, Keira continues to evolve, showing that she is as much an artist as she is an actress.

6.3 Challenging Projects

Keira Knightley's career is marked by her willingness to take on difficult projects that test her as an actor, push her outside her comfort zone, and allow her to explore complex characters and stories. These projects have not only demonstrated her versatility but also her commitment to making meaningful and thought-provoking performances. Whether tackling difficult historical figures, complex emotional arcs, or unconventional narratives, Keira embraces parts that require risk and artistry, making her one of the most respected and fearless actresses of her age.

KEIRA KNIGHTLEY

One of the most challenging tasks of Keira's career was The Imitation Game (2014), where she played Joan Clarke, a brilliant mathematician and cryptanalyst during World War II. Joan's role in cracking the German Enigma code was important, but her work was often overshadowed by the male-dominated environment of Bletchley Park, and her sacrifices were significant. Keira's portrayal of Joan required her to mix intellectual strength with emotional vulnerability, capturing the frustrations of a woman whose brilliance was often dismissed due to her gender. The challenge of playing a real-life figure—one whose achievements were only later recognized—required Keira to delve into the nuances of Joan's quiet determination, winning her a second Academy Award nomination.

Another challenging project was her part in Colette (2018), where Keira portrayed the groundbreaking French author Sidonie-Gabrielle Colette. Colette's life was filled with rebellion, love, and personal and artistic battles, and Keira had to tap into the full complexity of the character. The part demanded not only a physical transformation—Keira spent considerable time learning how to embody Colette's distinctive persona—but also a deep emotional commitment. Colette was an icon of sexual freedom and literary prowess in an era when such qualities were considered unconventional for women. Keira had to bring both the confidence and vulnerability of this literary figure to life, a challenge that needed her to move beyond her usual roles to truly embody a woman ahead of her time.

In The Duchess (2008), Keira portrayed Georgiana Cavendish, the 18th-century Duchess of Devonshire, a part that required her to navigate a life filled with political intrigue, heartbreak, and personal sacrifice. The character's tumultuous marriage to the Duke, her political involvement, and her complicated love life required a performance that balanced emotional depth with historical context. Keira's ability to portray Georgiana's intelligence, passion, and personal turmoil showed her ability to handle the complexities of a woman trapped by her title, but fighting for her agency in an era where women were largely powerless.

Another example of Keira's embrace of challenging material is Never Let Me Go (2010), a haunting science-fiction drama in which she played Kathy, one of a group of young adults raised to be organ donors. Set in a dystopian alternate reality, Never Let Me Go is an exploration of fate, love, and loss in a world where the characters have no control over their fates. The film's emotional weight and Keira's portrayal of a character who is quietly resigned to her fate offered a unique challenge. Kathy's journey is one of self-realization and acceptance, and Keira's ability to express the character's quiet sadness, longing, and hope made the film a powerful exploration of human existence.

Keira's decision to take on these difficult roles shows her ability to choose projects that not only offer commercial success but also provide a platform for a deeper study of human experiences. Whether it's the emotional complexity of a historical figure, the vulnerability of a

KEIRA KNIGHTLEY

character facing a tragic fate, or the rebellious spirit of a literary icon, Keira approaches these parts with the same dedication, vulnerability, and authenticity. Through her work, Keira continues to show that acting is not just about playing a part but about delving into the complexities of the human soul, making her one of the most dynamic actresses in contemporary cinema.

CHAPTER 7: PERSONAL GROWTH

Keira Knightley's journey through personal growth is deeply intertwined with her career, her roles, and her changing sense of self. Over the years, Keira has not only matured as an actress but also as a person, developing a more nuanced knowledge of fame, relationships, and her place in the world. Her personal growth is mirrored in the varied roles she chooses, her approach to her public image, and the way she handles the pressures and challenges of life in the spotlight.

In the early years of her career, Keira was often seen as the young, carefree starlet in Hollywood—an image reinforced by her parts in Bend It Like Beckham (2002) and Pirates of the Caribbean (2003). However, the immense fame that came with these films put her under constant scrutiny, and as she grew, Keira began to question the expectations placed on her, both by the public and by the industry. She has been vocal about how, in her younger years, the demands of fame and public attention felt overwhelming. Over time, however, she learned to navigate the pressures with a more grounded viewpoint.

A key part of Keira's personal growth has been her ability to embrace privacy and control over her narrative. As her career progressed, she made a conscious decision to step away from the public eye in certain ways, carefully curating the aspects of her life that she wanted to share. She reportedly said that she wanted to avoid the "exhausting" nature of fame and instead focus on her work and her family. This choice to reclaim some level of control over her personal life marks a significant step in her growth as a person, showing a growing sense of self-awareness and confidence in her limits.

Motherhood has also played a key role in Keira's personal growth. When she became a mother in 2015, her outlook on life and work shifted. The arrival of her first daughter, Edie, and later her second, Delilah, brought new responsibilities and joys, but also a deeper understanding of what truly means to her. Keira has spoken candidly about how motherhood has changed her approach to her career, making her more selective about the parts she takes on and more focused on balancing her work with time for her family. It was also through motherhood that Keira began to feel a stronger sense of purpose in her advocacy for women's rights and gender equality, using her platform to speak out on topics like maternity leave and reproductive rights.

Keira's personal growth is also reflected in the evolution of her acting decisions. She has moved from playing roles of romantic heroines to embracing more complex, diverse characters, often portraying women who question societal expectations. Through roles in films like Colette (2018), The Imitation Game (2014), and Never Let Me Go (2010), Keira has taken on characters who are truly flawed, bold, and multifaceted, mirroring her ney of self-discovery. She has spoken about the value of portraying women who are not perfect but rather whose strength lies in their complexity and humanity. These decisions show not just her growth as an actress, but her increasing desire to connect with characters who

KEIRA KNIGHTLEY

are real, who struggle, and who evolve in meaningful ways.

In addition to her career growth, Keira has become more open about the challenges of mental health. She has shared her experiences with anxiety, particularly in dealing with the pressures of fame and the public eye, speaking out in support of others who fight with similar issues. By addressing these personal challenges, Keira has set an example of vulnerability and bravery, showing that growth often comes from acknowledging and confronting one's weaknesses.

As she continues to evolve both professionally and personally, Keira Knightley remains a powerful example of resilience and self-awareness. Her journey of personal growth—marked by a balance between family, career, privacy, and self-advocacy—has made her not only one of the most respected actresses of her age but also a woman who has learned to navigate the complexities of life with grace, purpose, and authenticity.

KEIRA KNIGHTLEY

7.1 Advocacy

Keira Knightley's advocacy work reflects her strong sense of social responsibility, her commitment to women's rights, and her desire to use her platform for positive change. Throughout her career, Keira has consistently spoken out on a range of issues, from gender equality to mental health, and her advocacy efforts show her desire to add to meaningful conversations and drive societal progress.

One of the most significant causes Keira supports is gender equality, especially in the context of the entertainment industry. As a famous actress in Hollywood, Keira has used her visibility to draw attention to the gender disparity that still exists, both in terms of representation and compensation. She has been vocal about the need for greater diversity in film and television, advocating for more parts that portray women as multifaceted, strong, and complicated. Keira's own career choices—portraying a wide range of female characters who defy stereotypes—have mirrored this commitment to challenging traditional gender norms. Through her parts in films like Colette (2018), where she plays the trailblazing French author, and The Imitation Game (2014), where she portrays Joan Clarke, Keira has championed the stories of women who have historically been underrepresented or misunderstood.

Keira is also a vocal supporter of women's reproductive rights. She has spoken out about the importance of access to healthcare and the need to protect women's rights to make decisions about their bodies. Her advocacy for reproductive rights is particularly timely in the face of shifting political climates and legislative challenges, where Keira's impact has been a powerful reminder of the need to protect the hard-won freedoms that many women have fought for. She has supported campaigns aimed at raising awareness about women's health issues and ensuring that women's opinions are heard in these important discussions.

Another cause Keira is passionate about is the value of paid parental leave. As a mother herself, Keira has experienced directly the challenges of balancing career and family life. She has been an outspoken advocate for paid parental leave policies that support both mothers and dads, recognizing that the ability to care for one's child without sacrificing financial security is important for a balanced, equitable society. By using her platform to raise awareness about these policies, Keira has drawn attention to the need for systemic change that allows parents to prioritize their families without fear of losing their income.

Keira has also been a vocal advocate for mental health understanding. She has openly discussed her struggles with anxiety, especially the pressures of fame and the public scrutiny that comes with being in the spotlight. By speaking openly about her experiences, Keira has helped to reduce the stigma surrounding mental health, encouraging others to seek help and support when needed. Her openness on the subject reflects her belief in the importance of addressing mental health problems and creating a culture of empathy and understanding. She has also supported various mental health organizations and initiatives, using her voice to bring attention to the importance of offering resources for those who are struggling.

In addition to her advocacy work on social and political problems, Keira is also committed to environmental sustainability. She has shown support for initiatives aimed at combating climate change and promoting eco-friendly practices, and she has publicly spoken about the need to make both the entertainment business and society at large more environmentally conscious. Whether it's through the fashion choices she makes on the red carpet or the eco-friendly projects she supports, Keira has used her visibility to advocate for a more sustainable future.

Keira Knightley's advocacy work underscores her belief in the power of using one's stage for good. She has become an important voice in the fight for gender equality, women's rights, mental health awareness, and environmental sustainability. Her commitment to these causes, coupled with her candidness and willingness to speak out, has not only shaped her public image but also made her a role model for others who are determined to make a difference in the world. Through her activism, Keira has proven that advocacy is not just about raising awareness but about driving real change—using both her job and her voice to create a more just, compassionate, and equitable society.

7.2 Fighting for Women's Rights and Equality

Keira Knightley's dedication to fighting for women's rights and gender equality is a core aspect of her advocacy work. Throughout her career, Keira has used her platform to speak out on issues affecting women, from the gender pay gap in the entertainment business to the fight for reproductive rights. Her outspoken support for women's rights, combined with her commitment to challenging societal norms, has made her a significant figure in the wider movement for gender equality.

KEIRA KNIGHTLEY

One of the most notable areas in which Keira has fought for women is in the entertainment industry. As a prominent actress in Hollywood, she has consistently highlighted the disparities that exist between men and women, especially in terms of representation, pay, and opportunity. Keira has been vocal about the importance of creating more diverse parts for women, saying that women in film should not be confined to the traditional roles of romantic interests or supporting characters. She has frequently stressed that women should be portrayed as complex, multidimensional characters, with their narratives and storylines, not simply defined by their relationships with men. Her work has reflected this advocacy, as she has carefully chosen roles that portray strong, independent women who defy societal expectations.

In addition to championing better representation for women in film, Keira has been an advocate for fair pay in the entertainment business. She has spoken out about the gender pay gap that continues in Hollywood, emphasizing the need for equal pay for equal work.

KEIRA KNIGHTLEY

Keira's own experiences in the business have made her acutely aware of the disparities, and she has used her voice to call for change. In 2018, she made headlines when she admitted that she had been paid significantly less than her male co-stars in films such as The Imitation Game (2014). By publicly addressing this problem, Keira not only drew attention to the persistent wage inequality faced by women in the industry but also encouraged other women to speak up about their own experiences.

Keira has also been an outspoken supporter of women's reproductive rights. She has supported campaigns and groups that fight for a woman's right to choose, emphasizing that decisions about reproductive health should remain personal and private. Keira has used her public platform to highlight the importance of protecting access to safe and legal abortions, especially in light of rising political challenges to reproductive rights in many parts of the world. Her advocacy on this issue is deeply personal—Keira has spoken about her own experiences with the medical system and how critical it is for women to have control over their bodies. She has been an active voice in raising awareness about how women's reproductive rights are often undermined and has spoken out against political efforts to limit access to reproductive healthcare.

Beyond the entertainment business and reproductive rights, Keira has also been a vocal advocate for broader gender equality. She has supported initiatives that fight for equal chances for women in the workplace, as well as those that work to end violence against women. Keira has long been committed to fighting toxic masculinity and discussing how gender stereotypes limit both women and men. She has been vocal about the importance of teaching young people about healthy relationships, consent, and respect, especially in the age of #MeToo. Keira thinks that societal change must come not only through policies but also through cultural shifts that challenge and dismantle harmful gender norms.

Keira's advocacy for women's rights is also noticeable in her personal choices, such as her decision to participate

KEIRA KNIGHTLEY

in campaigns like Time's Up, an initiative to fight sexual harassment in the workplace. She has been outspoken about the need for a systemic overhaul in how the entertainment business, and society as a whole, handles cases of harassment and discrimination. Her support of feminist movements is based on her belief that all women should have access to the same opportunities, freedoms, and protections, regardless of their background or circumstances.

Keira Knightley's ongoing commitment to fighting for women's rights and gender equality has made her a powerful voice in the drive for social change. She continues to question the status quo, both in her professional choices and in her public advocacy, using her platform to raise awareness, inspire action, and drive real change. Through her work, Keira has shown that true equality is not just about access to opportunities but about dismantling the systems that perpetuate gender inequalities and ensuring that women's opinions are heard and respected at every level of society.

KEIRA KNIGHTLEY

7.3 Balancing Mental Health and Public Life

Balancing mental health with public life is a challenge many celebrities face, and Keira Knightley has been open about her issues in managing the pressures of fame while prioritizing her mental well-being. As one of the most successful actresses of her age, Keira's life has been under constant public scrutiny, which can take a toll on anyone's mental health. Over the years, she has shared her experiences openly, shedding light on the realities of being in the public eye while navigating personal battles with anxiety, stress, and self-doubt.

Keira has been vocal about the mental health challenges she faced early in her career, especially the anxiety she experienced as her fame skyrocketed. The heavy media attention that followed her success in films like Pirates of the Caribbean and Bend It Like Beckham left her feeling vulnerable and overwhelmed. She has spoken about the difficulties of growing up in such a public environment and how it led to feelings of insecurity and

KEIRA KNIGHTLEY

pressure to keep a certain image. Keira has explained that the constant judgment and scrutiny of her looks, her relationships, and her every move made her feel exposed and anxious, leading to emotional burnout.

Keira's openness about her struggles with anxiety has been an important part of her journey toward better mental health. She has made it a goal to find ways to manage the demands of public life while taking care of her mental well-being. A key aspect of this has been her conscious choice to step back from the limelight when necessary. Keira has stressed the importance of taking breaks from work and media attention, acknowledging that time away from the public eye has been crucial for her mental health. By carefully choosing which events to attend and how much she shares publicly, Keira has been able to create a more manageable balance between her job and her personal life.

One important factor in Keira's method of balancing mental health with public life is her commitment to setting boundaries. She has consistently advocated for the right to privacy, especially when it comes to her family life. As a mother, Keira has been especially vocal about the need for a private space for herself and her children, drawing clear lines between her professional image and her personal life. By setting boundaries around her family and the media, she has protected her mental health, enabling her to focus on what truly means to her without feeling constantly exposed or judged.

In addition to setting boundaries, Keira has sought professional help to handle her mental health. She has spoken openly about getting therapy and recognizing the importance of mental health support in her life. Keira believes that seeking help is essential, especially for those in high-pressure industries like entertainment, where the stigma surrounding mental health can often prevent people from getting the support they need. Her candidness about her own experiences with therapy has encouraged others, especially those in the public eye, to prioritize their mental health without shame or fear of judgment.

KEIRA KNIGHTLEY

Keira's advocacy for mental health awareness is also seen in her participation in organizations and projects aimed at providing mental health resources for people from all walks of life. She has worked with organizations that promote mental well-being and raise awareness about issues like depression, anxiety, and the importance of self-care. By using her platform to talk about mental health openly, Keira has helped destigmatize the conversation, reminding her fans and peers that even those who seem to have it all can experience the same emotional struggles.

Through her journey, Keira has learned the importance of keeping a healthy work-life balance, taking care of her mental health, and protecting her boundaries from the pressures of fame. Her ability to speak openly about her battles with anxiety and the challenges of balancing public life with personal well-being has made her a relatable and inspiring figure. Keira's commitment to mental health advocacy and her openness in sharing her story have helped to normalize these talks, making it easier for others to seek help and take care of their mental health. By prioritizing her well-being, Keira continues to show that taking care of oneself is not just an act of self-preservation, but an important example for others, especially in an industry that often prioritizes success over personal health.

CHAPTER 8: LEGACY

Keira Knightley's legacy goes far beyond her remarkable performances on screen. Over the years, she has carved out a place for herself not only as one of the most talented actresses of her generation but also as a powerful advocate for change, especially in the realms of gender equality, mental health awareness, and women's rights. Her legacy is defined by her dedication to challenging societal norms, breaking barriers in Hollywood, and using her voice to bring attention to causes that matter deeply to her.

Keira's body of work, ranging from her breakthrough role in Bend It Like Beckham (2002) to her transformative performances in period dramas like Pride and Prejudice (2005) and Colette (2018), shows her extraordinary range and dedication as an actor. She has played a wide range of characters—women of strength, intellect, vulnerability, and resilience—often tackling parts that highlight complex, multifaceted women who defy traditional expectations. Through these characters, Keira has made a profound effect on how women are portrayed in cinema, bringing nuance and depth to parts that have historically been underserved or reduced to stereotypes. Her performances have set new standards for what it means to be a leading woman in film, inspiring future generations of actresses to seek out diverse, empowering parts.

Keira's legacy also lies in her advocacy for gender equality in the entertainment business. As one of the few women in Hollywood who has regularly used her platform to call out the disparities in pay, representation, and opportunity, Keira has been a trailblazer. Her outspoken support for equal pay for equal work and her vocal criticism of the gender pay gap in Hollywood has sparked important conversations about fairness in the film business. By speaking out about her own experiences with unequal compensation, Keira helped shine a light on a systemic problem that affects women across all industries, encouraging others to demand better representation and fairer treatment. Her

KEIRA KNIGHTLEY

commitment to creating a more equitable space for women in film is a cornerstone of her lasting effect on the industry.

Beyond her work in entertainment, Keira's support for women's rights and mental health has left an indelible mark. Through her public support of women's reproductive rights, paid parental leave, and efforts for gender equality, she has used her voice to support causes that promote societal change. Keira's candidness about her problems with mental health, including anxiety, has played a crucial role in reducing the stigma around mental health issues, especially for those in the public eye. Her openness in discussing the difficulties of fame and the pressures it brings has helped to create a space where more people feel safe talking about their mental health, especially in industries that often silence such struggles.

Keira's legacy also includes her approach to navigating fame with authenticity. In a world that constantly demands public figures to conform to certain images,

KEIRA KNIGHTLEY

Keira has stayed refreshingly honest about her desire for privacy, her struggles with public attention, and her commitment to staying true to herself. She has managed to keep a sense of normalcy in her life, balancing her career with motherhood and her advocacy work. Her ability to manage the demands of stardom while protecting her mental well-being and personal life has set an example for others who are navigating the pressures of fame.

Keira Knightley's impact is one of empowerment—both for herself and others. She has used her platform to question the status quo, pushing for greater representation of women in film, advocating for gender equality, and fighting for mental health awareness. Through her exceptional career and advocacy work, Keira has inspired countless individuals to embrace their strengths, question societal norms, and never stop fighting for a world that is more inclusive and just. Her influence will continue to resonate in the years to come, as she remains a strong symbol of talent, resilience, and activism.

KEIRA KNIGHTLEY

8.1 A Lasting Impact on Cinema

Keira Knightley's lasting effect on cinema is a testament to her incredible range as an actress and her commitment to reshaping the representation of women in film. Over the course of her career, she has challenged traditional norms, taken on complex and groundbreaking roles, and become an influential figure in Hollywood, leaving an indelible mark on the industry that stretches far beyond her acting abilities.

One of Keira's most profound contributions to cinema is her ability to portray multifaceted female characters who defy the typical archetypes often given to women in film. From the rebellious and determined footballer in Bend It Like Beckham (2002) to the fiercely independent and ambitious writer in Colette (2018), Keira has consistently chosen parts that highlight women's complexity, strength, and intelligence. These characters are not defined simply by their relationships with men or by their appearance—they are dynamic, self-driven individuals with their desires, struggles, and aspirations.

KEIRA KNIGHTLEY

In doing so, Keira has played a major part in expanding the narrative possibilities for women in cinema, proving that women can be the protagonists of their own stories, not just side characters or romantic interests.

Keira's work in period dramas, especially in adaptations of classic literature like Pride and Prejudice (2005) and Atonement (2007), has also made a lasting impact on how women are depicted in historical films. These roles allowed her to breathe new life into famous literary characters, bringing a modern sensibility to portrayals of women from different eras. Her portrayal of Elizabeth Bennet in Pride and Prejudice is widely regarded as one of the most memorable in cinematic history, as Keira infused the character with intelligence, wit, and a sense of agency that had not always been stressed in previous adaptations. Through such performances, Keira has redefined the role of women in period dramas, showing that these characters can be more than just passive observers of history—they can actively shape their fates.

KEIRA KNIGHTLEY

Her work in the Pirates of the Caribbean franchise also had a major cultural effect, especially in the context of blockbuster filmmaking. As Elizabeth Swann, Keira not only brought depth and complexity to a character that was initially seen as a traditional damsel-in-distress, but she also became one of the key players in a global series that centered around male-led action. Elizabeth's development from a young, innocent aristocrat into a fierce and capable pirate was groundbreaking, helping to establish Keira as a strong female action hero who could hold her own alongside the likes of Johnny Depp and Orlando Bloom. Her portrayal helped to set a standard for stronger, more empowered women in action films, something that has since been echoed in other big franchises like The Hunger Games and Wonder Woman.

In addition to her impactful performances, Keira has added to a broader shift in the kinds of stories told in Hollywood. Her willingness to take on roles in smaller, independent films alongside big-budget blockbusters has helped diversify the types of films she participates in, further showing that an actress can work across genres

KEIRA KNIGHTLEY

and still maintain a powerful presence. Keira's participation in thought-provoking films like The Imitation Game (2014), Never Let Me Go (2010), and Seeking a Friend for the End of the World (2012) shows her ability to navigate both high-profile roles and deeply personal, challenging projects. These choices not only showcase her range but also contribute to a more varied and inclusive environment in film, where diverse voices and stories are given a platform.

Keira's advocacy for gender equality in Hollywood, especially her calls for better representation and fairer pay for women, has had a ripple effect on the industry. By openly discussing the gender pay gap and the challenges she faced early in her career, Keira has contributed to a bigger conversation about equity in film. She has constantly pushed for the portrayal of women as equals to their male counterparts, both on and off the screen. Her activism has played a part in the ongoing push for systemic changes in the film industry, where greater chances for women—both in front of and behind the camera—are becoming more visible.

Keira's effect on cinema is not only felt in the roles she has played but also in the way she has used her platform to influence and inspire the industry. Through her multifaceted career, her advocacy for women's rights, and her commitment to portraying complex female characters, Keira Knightley has left a lasting imprint on the way women are represented in film, ensuring that her influence will be felt by future generations of filmmakers, actors, and audiences alike.

8.2 Inspiring the Upcoming Generations

Keira Knightley's influence extends far beyond the films she's starred in; her career and advocacy have inspired countless young people, especially women, to follow their goals and challenge societal expectations. Her multifaceted journey as an actress, activist, and public figure has created a legacy that will surely inspire future generations to embrace their voices and break through barriers in their careers and lives.

KEIRA KNIGHTLEY

One of the most inspiring aspects of Keira's career is her ability to stay true to herself in an industry that often demands conformity. From a young age, she has taken control of her career, choosing parts that reflect her values, whether that's playing strong, independent women or tackling projects that challenge traditional gender roles. In an industry that has often relegated women to the sidelines or pigeonholed them into stereotypical roles, Keira has carved a path that values depth and complexity over superficiality. Her refusal to play only traditional "leading lady" parts, especially in her early career, has encouraged young actresses to seek out more diverse and empowering characters that allow them to showcase their range and challenge the status quo.

Keira's support for gender equality and women's rights is another source of inspiration for upcoming generations. She has consistently used her platform to speak out against the gender pay gap, demand equal representation for women, and support the rights of women to make decisions about their bodies. By being outspoken about these problems, Keira has shown that being in the spotlight comes with a responsibility to stand up for what's right. She has not only been a vocal advocate for the rights of women but has also been a role model for young women who may feel that they, too, have to conform to business standards or be quiet in the face of inequality. Keira's example shows that it's possible to succeed on your terms, using both your career and your voice to push for a better, more just world.

Her advocacy for mental health has also resonated strongly with young people, especially in today's increasingly stressful and interconnected world. By being open about her struggles with anxiety and the pressures of fame, Keira has helped to normalize conversations about mental health, inspiring others to seek help and value their well-being. She has shown that mental health should not be a taboo subject and that it's okay to talk about weaknesses, even for those who are in the public eye. Her honesty provides a model for young people to embrace their emotions, seek help when necessary, and take the time to care for themselves in a world that often prioritizes productivity over mental wellness.

Keira's influence is also felt in her portrayal of strong, independent women in film—characters who aren't defined by their relationships with men but by their ambitions, strengths, and personal journeys. For young girls and women watching her pictures, Keira has become a symbol of empowerment. Roles like Elizabeth Bennet in Pride and Prejudice, Joan Clarke in The Imitation Game, and Colette in Colette offer young viewers complex, multi-dimensional women who make their own choices, break through social barriers, and carve their paths. These characters inspire young people, especially young women, to realize their potential and pursue careers, interests, and lives that defy conventional expectations.

Keira's ability to juggle fame with a grounded personal life has also pushed many to approach success with balance. In an industry that often glorifies hustle and

KEIRA KNIGHTLEY

perfection, Keira has proven that it's possible to keep a sense of privacy, authenticity, and normalcy while achieving great success. She has been clear about her need for limits and space, especially when it comes to her family, which has encouraged many to think about the importance of balancing ambition with personal happiness and well-being.

As an advocate, actress, and role model, Keira Knightley's journey continues to inspire young people, especially women, to question societal norms, embrace their individuality, and use their platform for good. Her legacy is one of empowerment—showing that success isn't just about awards and fame, but about staying true to oneself, fighting for what's right, and uplifting others along the way. For the next generation of actors, activists, and everyday people, Keira's career offers both a blueprint for success and a strong reminder that our voices have the power to create change.

CONCLUSION

In conclusion, the journey of Keira Knightley stands as a testament to the resilience, ability, and authenticity of a woman who has carved out a place for herself as both a Hollywood icon and a champion for important causes. From her humble beginnings in the suburbs of London to her rise as one of the most famous actors of her generation, Keira's story is one of hard work, determination, and unwavering commitment to both her craft and her values. Her ability to navigate the pressures of fame while keeping a sense of self and standing up for what she believes in has made her a role model for countless people around the world.

Keira's legacy is defined not only by her remarkable performances in a diverse range of films but also by her willingness to break barriers in an industry that has long been ruled by rigid expectations. From her iconic parts in period dramas to her unforgettable portrayal of Elizabeth Swann in the Pirates of the Caribbean franchise, Keira

KEIRA KNIGHTLEY

has redefined what it means to be a leading woman in film. She has embraced characters that challenge the norms of femininity, bringing depth, intelligence, and complexity to every part she takes on. Through her work, she has shown that women can be strong, multifaceted, and unapologetically themselves—traits that have inspired generations of young actresses to follow in her path.

But Keira's impact goes far beyond her acting. She has used her platform to fight for gender equality, women's rights, and mental health awareness, issues that are particularly close to her heart. By speaking out about the gender pay gap, the need for more diverse representation, and the value of prioritizing mental well-being, Keira has become a powerful voice for change. Her advocacy for women's rights and her openness about her battles with anxiety have made her a beacon of hope for those who feel silenced or marginalized. She has shown that being vulnerable, taking care of oneself, and working for justice are not signs of weakness but powerful acts of strength.

KEIRA KNIGHTLEY

Keira's personal life has also been an important part of her story. As a mother and a wife, she has managed to find a balance between the demands of her work and the love she holds for her family. Her commitment to privacy, her efforts to protect her loved ones from the relentless scrutiny of the media, and her ability to keep a sense of normalcy in an often chaotic industry have set an example for others in the public eye. Through it all, Keira has stayed grounded and authentic—an inspiration to both her fans and peers alike.

Ultimately, Keira Knightley's life and work represent a journey of continuous growth, empowerment, and unapologetic authenticity. She has used her fame not only to fuel her success in Hollywood but to fight for the causes she believes in, inspire others to follow their passions and challenge the status quo. Through her portrayal of unforgettable characters, her groundbreaking work as an activist, and her unwavering commitment to staying true to herself, Keira has left an indelible mark on the world of film and beyond.

KEIRA KNIGHTLEY

As the years go by, Keira Knightley's legacy will surely continue to shape the industry she helped redefine, inspire the next generation of actors and activists, and stand as a powerful reminder that talent, integrity, and love can indeed change the world. Her journey is far from over, and as she moves forward, one thing remains certain: Keira Knightley will continue to shine as a beacon of creativity, passion, and compassion, inspiring those who dare to follow their paths, regardless of the hurdles they may face.

Printed in Great Britain
by Amazon